HIRING RIGHT

Getting the right people into our schools.

Dr. Abimbola Banu-Ogundere

Introduction

Great teams make greatness.

Great teams don't just happen; they are crafted intentionally.

The first step to crafting a great team is to hire the right

people.

~ Dr. Abimbola Banu -Ogundere

Every school leader's overarching goal is to build a great school.

As a school leader, your primary task is to create a great and competent team that can help you build a great school, and this starts with the question, "How do I get the right people into our schools?"

Having the right people on board doing the right things is in everyone's interest. Schools should be filled with people who are mission doers that can help the school attain its goals. Many of us focus more on developing programs, but programs do not make great things happen in schools; people do.

As a School leader, you should see staff openings as an opportunity for personal growth, the growth of your school, and a move towards ultimate greatness for your school.

Good leaders know that they are only as good as good as their team. The quickest way to improve our schools is to hire great teachers at every opportunity. The goal should be to hire people who the school can become like; people who are greater and better people than our current staff profile and who the school can learn best practices from. If this is not the goal or our outcome, then we are hiring the wrong people. It is impossible to improve a school by hiring people who fit right in with our average teachers.

As a School leader, you should seize the opportunities the Hiring process provides by paying the utmost attention to it.

With all that said, let's dive into how, using these TEN STEPS!

TEN STEPS TO HIRING RIGHT!

STEP 1:

CLARITY OF THE SCHOOL'S VISION AND MISSION

Our Vision for our school is our Guiding compass! Our true north!

Our vision should be authentic to us and informed by our history, experiences, preexisting environment, purpose and passion. Our own, not that of others.

With clarity of vision we know where we are going and are better able to outline how we want to get there.

Our vision must inspire us to take action and guide all the actions especially hiring. Great leaders are not only visionary, they are also architects who understand the role of people in the building process and commit fully to hiring people who are able and willing to help the school attain its vision. When we fail to hire in alignment with our vision, we are only paying lip service to our vision.

STEP 2:

DEFINE THE ROLES NEEDED FOR THE SCHOOL
TO ATTAIN ITS VISION.

When we are clear about where we are going, how we plan to get there becomes clearer and the roles needed become clear as well. The roles come first before the people. A school that intends to be the foremost school for digital technology in a country needs an expert or two in digital technology. Next step is to create a job description that outlines what this expert in digital technology is actually going to be doing in order to move the school closer to its vision.

STEP 3:

CREATE A JOB DESCRIPTION FOR EACH ROLE.

The job description details the duties which staff occupying each role must carry out in the school. It typically specifies;

- ⬚ Job title
- ⬚ Who the job holder is responsible to
- ⬚ Who the job holder is responsible for
- ⬚ Purpose of the job or main objectives to be achieved by the post holder
- ⬚ Main activities; what the post holder will do to achieve the objectives daily, weekly, monthly, and so on.

It's good to be as specific as possible.

The job description is used for identifying the selection criteria when shortlisting candidates who have applied for a position in the school. It outlines the expectations the school has of the staff. It is also essential for appraisal and accountability processes, such as performance reviews in schools.

Always remember that it is about the job and not the person.

STEP 4:

CREATE A PERSON SPECIFICATION FOR EACH ROLE.

A person specification gives clarity on the profile of the ideal person that can get the job done. What type of person is needed to do the job as outlined in the job description? This information is obtained from data collected from relevant stakeholders, skills, experiences, and knowledge required to carry out each duty in the job description.

For example, for teachers, put into consideration requirements such as;

- Professional Teaching qualifications such as NCE, Bachelors in Education, PGCE, PGDE, Masters in Education for teachers
- Teaching experience
- Skills, including soft skills
- Personality
- Culture fit and contribution
- Subject content knowledge
- Digital skills which may include basic ability in Microsoft Office programs, G suite for Education, Curating, organizing and share digital resources,

Creating interactive video content, info graphics and posters and so on.

It is important to distinguish between essential and desirable requirements.

An essential requirement is one that enables the post-holder carry out the job effectively.

A desirable requirement is one that contributes to effective performance but is not essential.

These requirements are school-dependent and are based on the school's vision and mission. For example, an essential requirement for the teaching profession is a professional qualification to teach. A desirable requirement may be teaching experience and specific skills which are developed on the job.

Ensure you don't list requirements as essential when they are not strictly so, as there is a real danger of discrimination.

STEP 5:

RECRUIT EXPERTLY

Recruitment is the process of generating a pool of qualified candidates for a job.

Successful recruitment is based on

- ⬚ Your school's employer brand
- ⬚ Your school's recruitment process
- ⬚ Your school's recruitment methods.

Employer brand: The way your school's prospective applicants and employees perceive the school as an employer. A strong employer brand gives people a compelling reason to want to work in your school and remain there. All companies, including schools, have an employer brand. Not all employers realise how critical their employer brand is for attracting and retaining staff.

An organisation's brand is a strategy that permeates every aspect of talent management.

Ensure to:

- Assess your Employer brand
- Define your message
- Communicate your message loudly and clearly
- Evaluate the effect of the message

Recruitment process: Involves planning, job posting, and all the necessary communication that occurs all through the process.

<u>Planning</u>: Ask yourself questions such as;

- How much money do we have to spend on the recruitment process?
- How much time do we have to recruit for jobs?
- What is the size of the candidate pool required?
- What level job are we recruiting?

The answers to these initial questions help to determine the next steps.

<u>Job posting</u>: Create an attractive advertisement with a catchy headline and information about

- The job, the ideal person for it as stated the job description and person specification,
- Your employer brand, benefits of working with your school
- Next steps to take for interested persons, including the school's formal contact details

Communication: Effective communication is critical to success. With excellent communication, the applicants will be more likely to consider the school as an employer. They will speak more positively about the school to others.

Recruitment methods; includes all the means of sourcing candidates

Successful schools use both internal and external recruitment methods.

Internal recruitment methods include

- Job board/ posting system
- Recruitment database
- Internal advertisement
- Promotions and transfers.

The advantages of internal recruitment methods include

- Cost-effectiveness (recruits already know the school, its culture, and the school already has a performance data of applicants)
- Motivating staff. It's good always to think, "Is there someone on the team we can teach these skills to?"

Disadvantages of internal recruitment methods include

- It creates a vacancy that has to be filled.
- There is inherently a lack of change.
- Employees who are not selected at the end of the process may feel disgruntled and upset at the system.

External recruitment methods include

- Advertising
- Direct mail
- Campus recruiting
- Job fairs
- Associations
- Employment agencies
- Internships

- Employee referrals
- Former applicants

Advantages of external recruitment include

- The infusion of new ideas and skills
- Change
- A diverse workforce into the school.

Disadvantages of external recruitment include

- Cost: external recruitment can be more expensive,
- Lack of knowledge of the recruits' performance data
- The possibility of internal resentment from existing staff.

A school should always explore these advantages and disadvantages thoroughly before deciding on which recruitment methods they would like to use. Schools should also be sensitive to the times when newness is needed in the faculty.

STEP 6:

REVIEW APPLICATION

This process is a crucial stage. Shortlisting the wrong candidates at this initial stage of selection will negatively impact the whole process. Paying attention to the presentation of the application at the expense of its content is a common mistake.

The content of the application can be compared to the selection criteria. The selection criteria can be made into a checklist using the information in the job description and person specification of the job, created based on the vision and mission of the school. All our actions must always serve our vision.

How does the person match up to the job description and person specification?

A scoring scheme where each criterion is scored from 1 to 10 can be created as a decision aid.

With scoring schemes, selectors/reviewers should

- Try to use the full length of the scoring scale (ready to award 0 out of 10 or 10 out of 10 if the candidate deserves it, rather than just clustering scores within a narrower range)

- Try to mark each criterion separately rather than mark on their general feeling about the candidate. With each criterion, they should ask, "What evidence have we got of the candidate's ability in this area?" and base their score on that evidence.
- Score independently, if there are more than selectors.
- Try not to be swayed by any special pleading on the part of the other selectors.

Sum up scores and invite the highest-scoring candidates for the next steps. Retain a record of the scores as evidence of how the school accepted/ rejected individual candidates.

Send an email to the shortlisted candidates inviting them for the next selection phase using a professional email address. Schools should not use personal email address to send official communication.

Transparency of the selection process is a vital management principle at this stage. It is good practice that candidates should receive as much information as possible about the selection process and how the organisation will reach its decision. Is there going to be a group test, what type of test is it going to be? How long will it last? Is there going to be a panel? Who are the members of the panel?

STEP 7:

CARRY OUT INITIAL TESTS

Shortlisted candidates should sit for timed tests that will assess their subject content knowledge of in subjects relevant to their roles—for example, Mathematics, Science, English, Social studies, and so on for Primary teachers, Aspects of effective operations for an Operations manager, Aspects of customer service for a customer service representative and so on. Tests can be paper-based or computer-based which also helps to assess the candidate's basic computer skills.

Include essay questions that help assess the candidate's critical thinking, problem solving, creativity, service orientation as well as writing skills.

Decide on a pass mark, below which candidates will not be considered for the role for example 75% and above. Shortlist candidates who score above pass mark.

The school can also use commercially available ability and psychometric tests such as:

- Personality Profiling.
- The Myers-Briggs Type Indicator.

- Sixteen Personality Factor Questionnaire.
- DISC
- Verbal Reasoning Assessment.
- Numerical Reasoning Assessment.
- Situational Judgement Test.
- Logical Reasoning Assessment.

These tests have gone through a rigorous process of test development so that test results are highly reliable. They are accompanied by test manuals that give explicit instructions on how the tests should or should not be used. They also include information about the relative performance of women and men, which the selector can use to help interpret test results and avoid discrimination.

Send an email to the candidates who pass the test inviting them for a panel interview. Send notification to those who didn't.

STEP 8:

SET UP PANEL SESSION

Candidates may sit before a panel made up of persons representing the school's stakeholders. This may include parents, governing body, teachers, or management who must all subject themselves to focus on what is best for the school.

The panel session may take place in a relaxed, formal, or semi-formal setting in the school. Some schools also opt for more casual and relaxed peer evaluation over lunch with candidates.

The panelists ask questions that assess candidates in areas that include but not limited to

- ☐ Knowledge of Vision of the school
- ☐ Passion and Enthusiasm for the job
- ☐ School Values
- ☐ Culture fit and contribution
- ☐ Professionalism
- ☐ Pedagogical knowledge
- ☐ Skills
  - ✓ Oral communication skills

- ✓ Creativity,
- ✓ Communication,
- ✓ Collaboration
- ✓ Organisation
- ✓ Judgement and Decision making
- ✓ Service orientation

Including teachers in the selection process allows them to be involved in the decision-making process. Include someone on the panel whose job is to sell the job to the candidates by sharing personal growth experiences and other benefits of working at the school.

Each panel member makes an independent assessment of the candidate without discussing it with other panelists using a scoring sheet and written observation.

Collate feedback from the panelists, and the candidates who have made the best impression across board are selected.

The panelists then go into a debriefing round table session where each selected candidate is discussed extensively, and the panelists arrive at a shortlist of the most preferred candidates.

Send mails to shortlisted candidates inviting them for the next step within 24 hours. Send mails to notify candidates who were not shortlisted.

STEP 9:

INVITE CANDIDATES FOR OBSERVATION

Invite shortlisted candidates to the school for a period of observation lasting one to three days or more, depending on what each school decides to do.

During this period, the candidate and the school are both checking for culture fit. It also allows the candidates to check if they would like to be part of the school. Remember, this is a joining of two entities that must come into the union with as much understanding of what they are getting into, as possible.

The school uses this opportunity to assess

- Personality
- Professionalism especially with regards to punctuality, appearance, teacher-child relationship, teacher-teacher relationship and so on
- Teaching skills through lesson observation, if they are teachers.

Candidates are shortlisted, based on feedback from observation reports submitted by staff members who act as observer.

Send mails to both shortlisted candidates and those not shortlisted.

STEP 10:

SET UP AN INTERVIEW WITH THE HEAD

Before meeting the Head, the personnel in charge of the hiring process such as Human resources manager or school administration should meet with the shortlisted candidates to discuss remuneration. Renumeration should be based on clear determinants, fair, motivating and include all benefits that accrue to the job.

The candidate also completes a **"Strengths finder"** questionnaire which helps the school to better understand what the individuals have to offer and how they can complement the needs of the team they will be working with.

The Human resources manager presents all the shortlisted candidates' documents to the School leader whose responsibility is to make the final decision through an interview of shortlisted candidates.

An Interview is a conversation with a purpose. It is a meeting lasting from 15 minutes to one hour between an employer or their representatives, who ask questions and a candidate who answers them. Candidates should also be allowed to ask questions to which the interviewer gives clear and accurate responses.

It is essential to use a consistent structure for the interview process to ensure consistency of candidate experience.

Here is a sample structure;

- Opening; Greetings and pleasantries exchange
- Experience questions to confirm background.
- Self-evaluation question to encourage candidate self-reflection.
- Behavioural question to assess past job performance.
- Questions from candidate and closing.

With interviews, it is important to:

- Ensure interviewers are not biased by features such as candidates' sex or appearance.
- Ensure interviewers have the skills of eliciting information from the candidate
- Ensure interviewers do not make premature judgements about the candidates.

Interviewers ask questions, lean into their instincts and experience, and use data collected from the selection process to decide on the best person for the job.

Interviewers should check for coachability, emotional intelligence, motivation, and temperament.

They must remember that what is paramount is what the candidate can genuinely contribute to the school's development rather than how the person conforms to the particular square hole needed to be filled at the time.

The interviewer informs the Human Resources manager/ School Administrator about candidates to be employed.

He or she sends a congratulatory email, offer of employment letter including responsibilities, probation period, benefits and start date to the shortlisted candidates.

The candidates who were not selected should also be notified.

What's next?

- ☐ Newly employed staff begin a probationary period which must begin with effective Onboarding. They should submit letters from their guarantors, proof of residence and national identity.

- ☐ During this period, school should start reference checks on newly employed staff. The right place to start is the previous jobs of the candidates. Send the schools an email. Ask nicely for a prompt response. Give about 5 to 7 days for a response. Check social media pages. Carry out Police checks to obtain police reports for each candidate.

You may need to be prepared to take the risk of overstaffing if a particular recruitment process produces two outstanding candidates for a position.

Financial constraints mean this is not possible in all circumstances. Still, there is evidence to show this approach pays dividends in the longer term.

School leaders should also not be afraid to start over again if a suitable candidate fails to materialize.

Finally,

Hiring the wrong people Is the fastest way to undermine a sustainable business. – Kevin J Donaldson

APPENDIX 1

SAMPLE JOB DESCRIPTION FOR A TEACHER

Job Title: Class Teacher

School: Junior & Senior School

Status: Full Time

Reports to: Key Stage Leader

No. of Direct Reports: 2

SUMMARY

The Class Teacher is responsible for teaching designated class pupils and ensuring that they achieve the highest possible standards of academic work and personal conduct in line with the school vision, mission, values and curriculum.

CORE RESPONSIBILITIES

Teaching

☐ Implement academic policies and the school curriculum to ensure pupils receive the highest standards of education

- Ensure high knowledge of related subjects and curriculum content
- Create weekly lesson plans in line with the scheme of work
- With support from Assistant Teacher (where applicable), prepare learning materials
- Follow the class timetable to create structure around lessons and daily class activities
- Teach pupils related subjects using a variety of lesson delivery methods
- Give regular class work and homework to assess how learning objectives are being met
- Ensure pupils' classwork and homework is marked
- Continuously track and record individual pupils' performance and progress
- Ensure pupils receive regular feedback on improvement areas and progress
- Uphold our school policies on pupils
- Promote personal and social development of class pupils and foster positive attitudes among them
- Track pupils during enrichment programs

- Be aware of and make provision for students who are AEN/SEN, very able, LAC or who have particular individual development needs
- Create a conducive and stimulating environment for teaching and learning by:
    - Ensuring board and classroom displays reflect concepts that are being treated in class
    - Ensuring class room is neat and tidy
    - Ensuring pupils' health and safety within and outside the classroom and report any health and safety hazards to the Key Stage Leader or School Administrator

Leadership

- Manage and provide leadership and guidance to associate teachers and assistant teachers (where applicable)
- Communicate curriculum, lesson plans and activities to associate and assistant teachers

- Work with Human Resources and Key Stage Leaders to evaluate performance of associate and assistant teachers
- Identify skill deficiencies in teachers and propose appropriate training
- Take responsibility for the effective, efficient and safe use of learning resources and equipment
- Take responsibility for own professional development

Reporting

- Prepare weekly lesson plans and submit on time
- Prepare weekly progress reports on academic, social and extra curricula activities and send to Key Stage Leader

Relationship with Parents

- Uphold our school policies on Parents
- Coordinate class parent-teacher conferences
- Ensure parents receive regular feedback about their children's progress and emerging needs

Daily Responsibilities

- Check to ensure class in conducive with regards to safety
- Check to ensure that all learning materials are ready for the day
- Receive pupils
- Check class attendance and report absences
- Ensure class timetables are adhered to
- Teach pupils related subjects
- Ensure homework for the day (if any) is given to all class pupils
- Ensure all class notes and previous day's homework is marked
- Ensure learning materials, classwork and homework for the following day is ready

Weekly Responsibilities

- Prepare weekly lesson planners and submit to Key Stage Leader
- Communicate approved weekly lesson planners to associate and assistant class teachers

- Oversee planned activities (field trips, special events/programs) for the week
- Prepare and submit weekly situation reports to Key Stage Leader

Monthly Responsibilities

- Review and discuss planned activities for the month

PERSON SPECIFICATION

- Minimum Bachelors' Degree in Education or PGDE
- Minimum 2 -6 years' experience as a teacher
- Excellent oral and written communication skills
- Knowledge of the primary school curriculum
- A high level of self-motivation and strong interpersonal skills
- Ability to uphold and model the school values
- Comfortable working independently and as part of a team
- Good leadership skills and ability to coordinate team to achieve set objectives
- Good problem solving and decision-making skills

- Ability to develop and maintain positive relationships with children and adults
- Positive attitude and enthusiasm
- Evidence of personal commitment to professional development
- Good organizational skills and the ability to effectively prioritize tasks
- Excellence in service delivery, focus on quality and attention to detail

You may be required to carry out other duties which may arise from time to time

APPENDIX 2

SAMPLE JOB POSTING FOR A TEACHER

Join an Amazing Faculty today!

A leading Nursery and Primary school in Lagos, Nigeria seeks to add to its exciting and vibrant faculty, passionate, enthusiastic, skilled and professional English teachers who are interested in working in an empowering and caring learning community with ample opportunity for career growth and development.

All applicants must

- Have a Bachelor's degree in Education
- Speak English language fluently
- Have very strong verbal and written communication skills
- Be skilled at using technology to foster learning
- Have at least three years of relevant and commendable work experience working with the British curriculum
- Be registered with Teachers' Registration Council of Nigeria (TRCN)

Interested applicants should send their application letter and most recent curriculum vitae to Human Resource Manager careers@theschool.com * before the 31st of June 2020.

APPENDIX 3

SAMPLE INTERVIEW QUESTIONS FOR TEACHERS

- What do you know about your subject? What do you like about your subject?
- How do you manage your own professional growth?
- Teachers should have a great capacity for continuous learning. How do you ensure that you are continuously learn?
- How do you find resources around the world that you can share with your students?
- How do you share what you already know with students?
- How do you teach students to learn what you don't know?
- What do you think are the most important skills to teach your children?
- How do you teach students to solve problems?
- How do you assess standout work that is handed to you?
- What are your expectations for students to self-assess their work and publish for a wider audience?

- What is your contribution to your faculty?
- What is your global relationship?
- How would you describe your internet footprint?
- How do you make sure your students are on task?
- How do you give students an opportunity to contribute purposeful work to others?
- How do you manage your classroom?
- How do you teach students to manage their own learning? Teachers should teach students to "learn how to learn"
- How are you able to apply technology to fundamentally change the culture of the classroom?
- Share with me a pie chart of your current position showing how you allocate your time.
- Tell me about your team size and reporting structure
- How do you collaborate across your team?
- What does 'sense of urgency' mean to you in your current environment
- What is your preferred success measurement?
- Tell me about a time you disagreed with your line manager.

- Tell me about a time you found a child's behavior very challenging.

- What do you anticipate to be your biggest learning curve taking on this opportunity and how would you expect to manage it?

- Highlight for me your strongest skills that would enable you to hit the ground running.

- Share with me an unforgettable classroom experience.

- Share with me some of the ways you have ensured that each parent receives an enjoyable experience in the school.

- How would your last supervisor describe you in three words.

- You are interviewing this school as much as we are interviewing you. What questions do you have for me?

APPENDIX 4

<u>Interview questions for Key Stage Leaders for Internal hiring</u>

<u>SELF</u>

- Why do you think you have been chosen to interview for this role?
- How would you describe your experience so far at our school using ONE WORD?
- Explain a significant factor that has supported your personal growth at our school since you joined
- Discuss a major challenge you have faced during your stay at our school and how you overcame it.
- Who is your role model? Explain how this person's life has inspired you.
- This new role entails leading beyond the classroom whilst still meeting the teaching and learning needs of your classroom. How do you intend to increase your capacity to handle such a role?
- You have to teach and assess a class with 18 children yet you have a deadline to submit an important report to the Director before the close of work. How

would you go about meeting these competing demands?

Our School

- What is the vision of our school? How would you explain to a new member of your team, their role in the school's attainment of this vision?
- What three factors in your own opinion have contributed most significantly to the success of our school?
- What are your aspirations for our school?
- Explain three opportunities you think there are for the school and how you think the school can harness these opportunities.
- Describe '(insert school name) School' child.

Teaching and learning

- What do you understand by the phrase 'Every Child Matters'?
- Safe guarding children is an important part of the work of every teacher. Please give some examples of

how you would make our school a safer environment for children.

- ⁇ What in your opinion are the keys to high quality teaching and learning?
- ⁇ How would you go about improving morals and character amongst the children in your key stage?
- ⁇ What are the 21st century success skills? Why are they important? Explain how you would foster one of them amongst your children in the Key stage.

Team

- ⁇ Nature vs Nurture? Explain
- ⁇ How would you support your team to achieve superior performance?
- ⁇ How would you handle an underperforming team member who is your friend?
- ⁇ What in your opinion is the most significant role of a leader of a team?
- ⁇ Leading a team in our school. What are the challenges you foresee and how do you plan to mitigate them?

- Motivation. What are your thoughts about motivation? How would you go about motivating your team mates? How do you keep yourself motivated?
- How would you deal with a difficult supervisor/ line manager?
- You have just given an instruction to your team about how a task should be completed and the Head Teacher gives a conflicting instruction which your entire team has decided to obey. How would you salvage the situation?

Home-school partnerships

- What in your opinion is the importance of home-school partnerships? Explain three ways you would foster good home-school partnerships in your key stage.
- How would you deal with a situation where a child keeps coming to school with homework not done?
- How would you deal with a parent who is angry for legitimate reasons?

- What in your opinion are parents looking for in schools?

- You have been called upon to discuss with a prospective parent making enquiries about the school. What four things would you say to the parent about the school to convince them to enroll her child?

APPENDIX 5

LESSON OBSERVATION FORM

DATE: _____

CLASS: _____

SUBJECT: _____

TOPIC: _____

TEACHER: _____

Supervisor: _____

RATING

Scoring guide for each aspect of the lesson

4	Mastered
3	Strongly developing
2	Developing
1	Needs Attention

Areas to look at	Score	Score	Score
Clean & Tidy Class			
Class Displays connect with topic			
Lesson materials and			

stationery are ready for use before lesson begins			
Lesson objectives are communicated at the start of the lesson			
Effective hook used as starter			
Reference to previous learning/ knowledge			
Lesson activities effectively meet lesson objectives			
Subject content knowledge			
Simple and clear age appropriate explanations			
Intra- curricular links			
Cross curricular links			
Real life connections			
Effective and relevant instructional strategies			
Learning is improved and extended by Teacher's use of technology			
Questions foster critical			

thinking			
Adequate response time to is given to questions			
Teacher's tone is appropriate and support			
Differentiation is evident and supports learning			
Evidence of extended learning			
Teacher sets high expectations and communicates them clearly			
Learners work collaboratively			
Use of Formative assessment			
Use of positive reinforcement			
Effective use of feedback to improve learning outcome			
Learners were engaged in the lesson			
Lesson ends with a plenary and connection to next lesson.			

Structured lesson with good progression and pace. Learning time is maximized effectively.			
Lesson ends at the planned time.			
Teacher- Child relationship and class atmosphere are positive			
Classroom management techniques support learning			
SCORE	/120	/120	/120

	For all the children	For some children	For a few children
Did learning take place?			
Was the lesson suitably challenging?			

Scoring Guide for TOTAL SCORE OF lesson observation

Score	Rate Level	Rate Name
<40	1	Poor

40- 55	2	Fair
56-70	3	Satisfactory
71- 85	4	Good
>85	5	Impressive

Observers' comments including explanation od score using scoring guide, targets and teacher's progress along previously set targets.

APPENDIX 6

EMPLOYER BRAND

75% of job seekers consider an employer's brand before they even apply for a job—and companies are taking notice.

96% of employers believe that their employer brand and reputation can positively or negatively impact revenue. With numbers like these in mind, many organizations make efforts to build and strengthen their employer brand.

The question is: how can they measure how successful their employer branding program is?

It all comes down to tracking the right employer branding metrics—and we're here to share 11 of the best ones to help you measure your company's success. Keep reading to learn why they're important and how they're calculated!

Measuring metrics that match your recruitment goals

"Start with your goals. Without clear goals, you'll never be able to measure success. If your goal is to retain employees by adding a benefit package, your measure of success would be employee retention and feedback on that package. If your goal is to drive awareness, there's a metric for that. If your goal is to get clicks to job openings, there's a metric to that.

Set clear goals and measure against them." – Carmen Collins, Social Media & Talent Brand Lead, Cisco

In other words, there are no universal or one-size-fits-all employer branding metrics that every company should measure. The metrics you track are entirely dependent on the goals your company wants to achieve with building its employer brand. You have to know what you're trying to achieve to measure how successful you are in your efforts, right?

Some of the most common employer branding goals are:

- **Building a positive reputation as an employer.** A top goal for companies focusing on employer branding efforts is to build a reputation as an employer. This helps companies differentiate themselves from their competitors and demonstrate their unique mission, values, and culture.

- **Attracting high-quality candidates.** Of course, you want to attract top-quality candidates—and employer branding is a great way to do just that. Many employers focus on employer branding to reach the best candidates in the job market.

- **Decreasing the overall cost per hire.** A strong employer brand can help decrease your cost per hire significantly, by as much as 43% or higher. Companies with a positive reputation as an employer receive more applicants who are a better fit, ultimately decreasing the overall cost per hire.

Employer branding metrics to measure success

Hannah Fleishman, Inbound Recruiting Manager at Hubspot, explained why the employer branding metrics you track should align with your company's specific recruitment goals:

"Most companies I talk to about employer branding do one of two things: They measure everything, or they measure nothing. Tracking every email click-through-rate, web page view, and application conversion rate is a good idea in theory, but what does that actually tell you about the impact of your efforts? Pick metrics that you know you can have an impact on, but that also move the needle on your overall recruitment goals." –Hannah Fleishman, Hubspot

Here are 11 employer branding metrics that can help you measure the effectiveness of your efforts and the strength of your employer brand.

1. Candidate Quality
If you want to attract high-quality candidates, then you need to look into whether you're doing so. Studies show that a strong employer brand leads to 50% more qualified applicants, but how can recruiters measure and learn from candidate quality? Along with results of pre-employment assessments used to screen and evaluate applicants,

recruiters can calculate the percentage of applicants to interviews, which is around 12% on average.

If your applicants-to-interview ratio is above 12%, you're probably attracting a lot of qualified applicants to your company. If it is less than that, you should think about ways to improve candidate quality.

Number of applicants / Number of interviews

= Candidate Quality

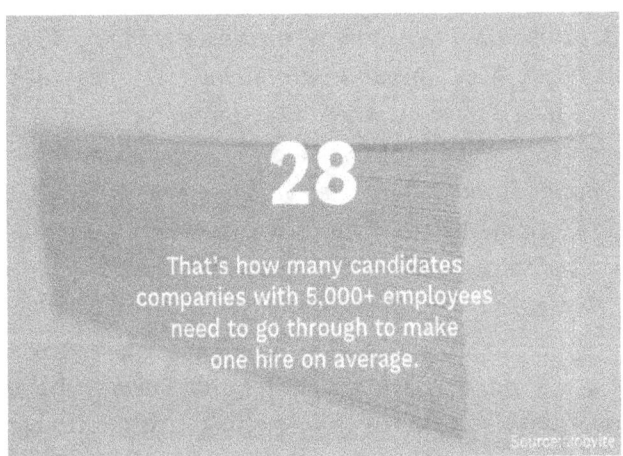

28

That's how many candidates companies with 5,000+ employees need to go through to make one hire on average.

Source: Jobvite

However, some roles attract as many as 250 candidates. The more quality candidates you have, the more choice you have and the more likely you are to make the right hiring decision.

2. Cost Per Hire

Fees for recruiting, pre-employment assessments, advertising, and more all contribute to the cost per hire—and it adds up quickly. As we mentioned before, a strong employer brand can help decrease your cost per hire significantly. (In fact, it some cases it nearly cuts the cost per hire in half!)

When a company earns a reputation for being a top employer, more candidates come to them directly—and those candidates are often a better fit for the organization since they know exactly what it stands for. With more quality candidates coming to them, recruiters can spend less time— and of course less money—on sourcing ideal people for open roles.

(Internal + External recruiting costs) / Total number of Hires = Cost per hire

3. Brand Awareness

While brand awareness is a bit more abstract than the more tangible employer branding metrics, it's really important to have an idea of how many people know you as an employer. The more well-known and well-liked your company is, the more likely it is you'll attract high-quality candidates when hiring, because you will be their employer of choice.

Rather than calculating a number with a formula, brand awareness can be measured through social listening. By monitoring your social media mentions and interactions, you can develop a better understanding of brand awareness and sentiment—meaning how people feel about your company as an employer.

17%

of companies have a clearly-defined strategy to strengthen their employer brand using social networks.

Source: Pagelip

...and 86% of job seekers use social media in their job search. That's why finding ways to raise your brand awareness through social media is key to strengthening your overall employer branding.

4. Source of Hire

Where did your hires come from? How did they find out about you? Measuring source of hire helps recruiters learn where they're most effective and what sourcing channels are less successful. To measure source of hire, determine where the bulk of your hires come from and evaluate whether you're allocating resources effectively.

If you recognize that very few of your new hires are coming from more cost-effective sources like employee referrals, you may want to consider strategies to increase referrals. For example, many companies offer referral bonuses to current employees who refer people for open roles.

Stop guessing, Start data-driven hiring.

5. Number of Open Applications

While this may not seem like a metric worth tracking, it's really helpful to track the number of candidates that apply for open roles. By adding this option to your career site, you can be sure that people who sent in an open application know your employer brand.

Studying the number of applications will also help you gain an understanding of how visible your company is as an employer. If you focus on building a strong employer brand and then begin to notice an uptick in the number of open applications coming in, you're probably on the right track.

6. Offer Acceptance Rate

Measuring the offer acceptance rate is beneficial to employers for so many reasons. Not only does it help track how successful your hiring efforts are, but also points out the number of candidates who are turning down offers. You can calculate the offer acceptance rate and complement it by researching the reasons for rejection. Ask for feedback and learn as much as you can about why you're not the employer of choice for candidates who reject your job offers.

Total offers made / Offers accepted = Offer acceptance rate

7. Hiring Manager Satisfaction

One of the best ways to measure the success of your employee branding program is to incite feedback from hiring managers. How satisfied are they with your candidate selection?

Measuring hiring manager satisfaction will help you determine whether or not you're attracting the candidates you aim to attract, as well as how good of a cultural fit they are. One way to measure hiring manager satisfaction is to send out surveys to learn how satisfied managers are with the candidates you're recruiting and analyze the feedback.

8. Employee Experience

A major aspect of employer branding is determining how well the employee experience matches up to what type of employer the company thinks they are. While there's no formula for calculating something like the employee experience, there are still ways you can measure and learn from it. Many companies analyze insights gleaned from employee surveys and exit interviews to get helpful feedback on the employee experience.

If you find out that your employee experience differs from what you're trying to provide as an employer, it might be time to make changes in how you're building and communicating your employer brand.

Companies that invest in employee experience are

4X

as profitable as those that don't.

Source: Employee Experience Advantage by Jacob Morgan

Companies investing in employee experience also outperform others in employee growth and average revenue.

9. Employee Referral Rate

A study revealed that while referrals only accounted for around 7% of applicants, they still generated over 40% of new hires. Employee referrals help decrease cost per hire and improve retention rates—so it goes without saying that many companies measure employee referral rates. By learning the number of employee referrals, you can better understand how effectively you're communicating your brand internally and externally.

10. Employee Retention Rate

Employees are always coming and going—especially in today's dynamic job market. Many of the companies looking for ways to reduce turnover and increase retention focus on building out their employer brand to make improvements.

Some studies suggest that retention rate is the most commonly measured employer branding metric, which makes sense because it's easy to measure and brings a lot of insights through conducting and learning from employee exit interviews. Find out as much as possible about your employees' experiences before they jump ship and use what you learn to improve your employer branding and recruiting processes.

11. Bonus Tip: External Reviews

In addition to these metrics, it's always a good idea to review and learn from your company's online presence. Websites like Glassdoor, Comparably and Indeed provide overall company ratings, CEO approval ratings, current and existing employee reviews, and many other helpful details that you can leverage to inform your company's employer branding strategy.

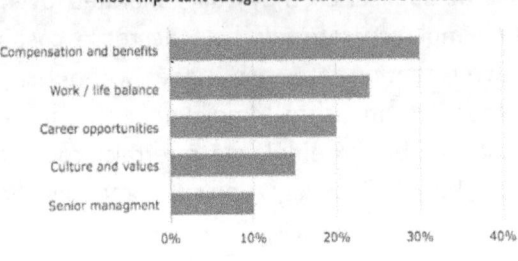

Most Important Categories to Have Positive Reviews

Almost half of job seekers indicate that they read company reviews in their job search. 30% of those look for positive reviews regarding compensation & benefits.

Wrapping it up

To measure the success of your employer brand, you need to determine the right combination of employer branding metrics that will help you further optimize your activities and track your goals over time. The 11 employer branding metrics we shared in this article should be a good place to start. Now check out these employer branding examples for retail and hospitality businesses for ideas on how to become an employer of choice!

(culled from harver, 11 Employer Branding Metrics To Measure Success @ https://harver.com/blog/employer-branding-metrics/)

Thank you for reading.

Please resend your reviews to aaogundere@gmail.com

Happy Hiring.

Dr. Abimbola Banu-Ogundere, 2020

www.ingramcontent.com/pod-product-compliance
Lightning Source LLC
Chambersburg PA
CBHW072146230526
45467CB00040B/665